D0841874

earth angels

EARTH ANGELS

CAROLYN HOLBROOK

SPOUT PRESS
MINNEAPOLIS, MN

Earth Angels
Carolyn Holbrook

ISBN 978-0-9835478-7-7

First Edition
Printed in the United States of America

Spout Press is a member of CLMP and is distributed to the trade
by Small Press Distribution, Berkeley, CA
(www.spdbooks.org)

Published by
Spout Press
P.O. Box 581067
Minneapolis, MN 55458-1067

"We go on with the dead inside us."

—Eve Joseph, *Yellow Taxi*

As I sit in my car waiting for the light to change, I cringe when I see a bus nearing the intersection of 28th and Lyndale. Whenever I close my eyes, I find myself back inside the moment when the dark-clad woman crashed onto the hood of my car, slid into the street, hit the pavement, bounced, then rolled into the gutter. It was two weeks ago but still I can't stop my hands or my body from shaking whenever I draw close to that intersection. I wish I could find another way to get to my office but even if I circle the block and take the next street over, I can't avoid it. Not really.

When the accident happened I felt like I was outside of my body, watching myself jump out of my car, leaving the door open and the engine running. It was almost as if I were someone else watching me run over to where the woman was lying, someone else watching me tear my coat off, plop down onto the curb and gently lay the woman's head in my lap and wrap my coat around her to keep her warm while we waited for the ambulance to arrive. She was so young, she could have been one of my daughters. I wanted to keep her safe, like I hoped someone would take care of my daughter if any such circumstances arose.

People soon appeared, seemingly out of nowhere, some to see what had happened, others to help. A man in a dark green hoodie and tan cargo shorts called 911. I wonder why I remember the details of what he had on but nothing about the woman who sat beside me and draped a blanket around my shoulders along with a comforting arm, or the man who gave me a flower or the person who turned off my car and handed me my keys?

A young officer with a blonde crew cut took the police report. With a kindness in his voice that surprised me, he said he wasn't going to ticket me. "This is a dark corner and she was dressed in dark clothing," he said. "I probably wouldn't have seen her either."

An ambulance snaked through the crowd, its siren making those intermittent chirps that warn people to make room so it can get through. While the EMTs strapped the woman to a backboard to place her inside the ambulance, I asked if I could accompany her to the hospital. One of them replied that they could only tell relatives which hospital they were taking her to. And then, as quickly as they arrived, they took off, siren blaring, leaving me standing in the street watching the crowd disperse into the night.

For a moment I wondered if I had been dreaming, but soon a middle-aged couple came over and helped me back into my coat. I had forgotten how chilly it was. It was March, and we were in that in-between stage where it might snow one day and you can wear a light jacket the next. I accepted their offer to take me home. The man helped me into my car and asked for directions, and the woman followed in their car.

Once home, I jabbed the elevator button several times, as though punching it might make it come faster. When I finally reached my apartment, I rushed to the phone before taking my coat off or putting my purse down and called Hennepin County Medical Center, Abbott Northwestern, North Memorial and Methodist Hospitals. None would give me any information. One receptionist said, "Lady, we get a lot of accidents in here every night. Unless you can give me the victim's name, there's nothing I can tell you." I wanted to go to each hospital and demand that they tell me if she was there but I knew it would be futile; I didn't know her name and doubted I could describe her. So I sat on my couch in a daze instead. After a while, I fell into a brief, restless sleep and woke up screaming, "Something's gone terribly wrong!"

I couldn't stop thinking about the accident over the next few days. Couldn't stop talking about it, either. I needed to know if the woman was all right. Friends and colleagues advised me to leave it alone. "She might sue you," they warned. But I couldn't leave it alone. My heart wouldn't be quiet, neither would the nightmares and daytime images of her limp body sliding off the hood of my car.

Early in the morning, three days later, the day the policeman said I could pick up a copy of the Police Report, I headed over to the precinct, which at that time was located on 24th and Nicollet. I hesitated before going in, fighting flashbacks of a night some years before when cops burst into my apartment looking for my son. The digital clock on my night stand showed 3:16 a.m. when I heard the hard, insistent knock. I jumped out of bed and ran to the door, sure that something horrible had happened. A look through the peephole revealed three beefy cops, each with a gun in the holster resting against his hip. A fourth man stood in front of them. I assumed he was a detective – he was wearing a suit that reminded me of the cheap grey suits I see on detectives in movies and *Law & Order* episodes.

I opened the door slightly, leaving the chain secure. My heart was pumping so hard that I could hear it. The detective, a short, slender man with graying brown hair flashed his badge and asked if my son was home. "No," I replied. But before I could tell him that Stevie had called a couple hours before and told me that he was in jail, having been mistaken for a guy who had committed a murder, the detective motioned to the others. They pushed past me and rushed into my apartment, snapping the chain on the lock.

"Wait, wait," I screamed. "Stevie's not here, he's in jail!" But by then they were storming through the apartment knocking my furniture over, scattering toys and tearing covers off beds, yelling "Where is he? Where the hell is he?"

My other four children, who were much younger than eighteen-year-old Stevie, were disoriented from having been wakened so harshly. They ran through the apartment like scared rabbits, screaming their little hearts out while they watched the gang of burly white men in blue uniforms and guns rage through our home.

Trying to stay calm, I picked up my youngest and placed her on my hip, and led the others who were clinging to me by then into my home office, my bare feet sloshing through a wet spot on the carpet where one of the girls had soiled her nightgown. I called the detective into the room, then picked up the phone, turned on the speaker option and dialed the Minneapolis Men's jail. I asked the man who answered if they were holding my son. The detective, clearly surprised by the response he heard from the other end of the phone, stopped his men. They left, leaving me to calm my children and to clean up the mess they had created. I never received an apology. Neither did Stevie.

I couldn't shake the memory off completely but didn't have much choice but to move it aside so I could get the police report. I stepped cautiously into the precinct office and stood at the counter watching the blue-uniformed men and women, some talking on the phone, others sitting at worn grey metal desks shuffling papers, until one of them, a white-haired man with a paunch, noticed me and granted my request.

Relieved that the police report showed that the woman was uninjured – just bruised and shaken – I rushed home, grateful that her name, address and phone number were on the document. I picked up the phone and punched in her number, rubbing my sweaty palms on my jeans while her phone rang. Her answering machine confirmed that I had dialed the right number, the number for Cassandra, the name on the police report. My lips parted but the words I wanted to say stayed glued inside of my mouth. I quietly placed the receiver back in its cradle and tried again an hour later. This time she answered on the second ring. Fearing that she might think it was a prank and hang up if I didn't say something soon, I let my words tumble out, telling her who I was and why I was calling. I listened to her inhale and exhale on the other end, sure that she was going to slam the phone down and probably change her number. But after a moment she said "I've been wondering how you're doing, too." That was the last thing I expected to hear.

I probably should have stayed home the night the accident happened. I hadn't been thinking clearly since my brother's leg was amputated two weeks before. But a dear friend was releasing a new chapbook that night and I wanted to soak in the awesome power of her poems and the soothing quality of her voice, hoping that it would ease my sadness. But I wasn't able to focus so I left early.

Thankfully, the reading was in the building where my office was located, in uptown Minneapolis's LynLake neighborhood, so I didn't have to think much about where I was going or finding my car after I left. I got into my car, circled the block, and headed toward 28th Street pretty much on autopilot. I turned onto 28th and was moving toward the left lane in order to turn onto Lyndale when a smell washed over me – that unmistakable odor of antiseptic mixed with the sweat of anxiety that pervades hospital waiting rooms everywhere and exudes from families who are waiting for the outcome of their loved one's surgery. I tried to stay focused on driving but the powerful smell took me back to the day of my brother's surgery.

The doctor came into the waiting room and

reported that the surgery had gone well. Relieved, my mother and her best friend and I were ushered into the recovery room. I watched Mama as she stood beside Ronnie's bed making small talk with the nurse tending to him. I've always admired my mother's ability to engage in small talk, something that I do not share. I was also deeply aware of the peace that had been growing between Mama and me over the last few years since my brother, Woody, and my sister, Joanne had passed away. The tension that characterized our relationship since I was a little girl seemed to have disappeared in the face of these losses. And now that Ronnie was ill, I was grateful for the harmony we shared.

Once Ronnie was cleared to be moved to the room that would be his home for the next week, we walked a few steps behind the aide who was rolling his gurney through the hallways.

We soon noticed that Ronnie was becoming agitated. Mama quickly moved to one side of him and I went to the other side. She reached over the siderail and rested her hand on his shoulder in an effort to comfort him but he started tearing at the sheet as though he wanted to jump off of the gurney and run. The aide was strong and able to contain him without much effort and Mama, though horrified, spoke to him calmly, words I do not recall. But I don't think I will ever forget the desperate sound in my brother's voice when he cried out through a medicated stupor, "Something's gone wrong! Something's gone terribly wrong!" I gripped the siderail tighter and watched my mother trying to hide the strain on her face. Her friend started praying, a prayer she continued all the way down the seemingly endless hallway until we reached his room.

Ronnie had been sick for years – first with schizophrenia, and then with diabetes, which eventually caused his legs to be amputated. This would have been tragic under any circumstances, but Ronnie was a classically trained dancer and choreographer. He had studied with the great Caribbean-born dancer/choreographer/ anthropologist, Pearl Primus, in New York in the 1960s. When he returned to Minneapolis, he taught African dance and drumming at The Way Opportunities Unlimited, Inc., a center in North Minneapolis that had been designed with a dual purpose: to help the city's Black residents feel pride in themselves, and to diffuse tensions after rebellions had broken out following the assassination of Dr. Martin Luther King, Jr. He had founded his own dance company, Feast Of the Circle Dancers and Drummers, and had taken them to West Africa and Haiti to learn from the masters and perform with them. And he had danced with the Minnesota Dance Theater. A striking photo once hung in their lobby – a brilliant photographer had snapped the shutter at the moment Ronnie reached the peak of a powerful ballet leap, making it look as though he were suspended in mid air. I have always admired my brother for his ability to accomplish so much with a serious mental illness, but his left leg was amputated a year ago and he had been in a nursing home ever since. And now his right leg was amputated, slamming the door shut and placing an exclamation point at the end of the dream he had held onto for so long, of someday dancing again.

Once Ronnie was settled into his room, Mama and I stood on either side of his bed, avoiding each other's gaze, forgetting about her friend who had found a chair and sat quietly out of the way. We both believed we needed to be strong for each other, but in truth, we were both as fragile as glass and could be shattered at any moment. We both feared that if we looked at each other, with even a small glance, the tears pooling behind our eyelids would erupt.

The next day, I sat beside my brother and watched him sleep; his skin, once the shade of black coffee, had turned ashen from the effects of the anesthesia, and his greying afro was in need of care. His deep, even breathing placed me in a kind of trance, easily enjoying childhood memories, memories of walking to school with my three siblings, all of us bundled up in parkas and woolen hats and scarves to shield us from the cold on winter days, or walking to St. Leonard's Catholic church, or Nicollet Park on hot summer mornings for day camp. Woody and Joanne, the older siblings, were charged with taking care of Ronnie and me while Mom did piecework at Honeywell or cleaned rich white women's homes during the day so she could afford to go to beauty school at night. Music played in my mind's ear with memories of us dancing around the house, Ronnie teaching me tap and ballet moves he learned at Billings & Betty dance school when we were 9 or 10 years old. Another memory almost made me laugh out loud – it was a hot summer day, and Joanne wanted to make peanut butter and jelly sandwiches for us to take to our summer program at Nicollet Park. She couldn't find the jelly, but there was Jell-O left over from the previous night's dessert. By lunch time, the Jell-O had melted and our sandwiches were a soggy mess.

When we were teenagers, Ronnie studied and performed at the Minneapolis Children's

Theater. One day he confided, with a certain pride in his voice, that the aging man who ran the theater wanted to be his boyfriend. I remember feeling horrified, not knowing what to do with this information. That night at dinner I looked around the table from Mama to Woody to Joanne to our stepfather, Barney, then back to Ronnie, who seemed all aglow. Would I spoil an enjoyable family moment if I said something? Would Ronnie feel betrayed? Would anyone even believe me? I decided to stay silent.

I sometimes wonder if Mom and Barney had any suspicions. I wondered even more after that man was publicly exposed years later, and convicted of child sexual abuse. But that day in the hospital, the day after Ronnie's surgery, my most pressing thought while watching him sleep was that it may not be long before he might be my third and final sibling to go to their grave. And indeed, heart failure and complications from his diabetes took his life two years later. Knowing that he was gay, several of my well-meaning friends said in their offerings of sympathy, "I know what you're going through, I had another friend who died of AIDS." At first I was shocked and then I was just plain pissed. Didn't these intelligent, caring people know that HIV/AIDS isn't the only cause of death for gay men?

With all of this going on in my mind, I know I was distracted the night of the accident. I felt so guilty that it was hard to believe this woman whom I might have killed said she had been wondering how I was doing since the accident. And yet, here she was, continuing the pattern of kindness that so many people had shown me that night. I wanted to tell her the truth, that I wasn't doing very well, that in addition to Ronnie's recent surgery, I had lost two of my siblings over the last eight years.

I wanted to tell her about the night my sister told me she was getting married, a week or two after telling me she was afraid of her fiancé. He had been verbally abusive in the year they had been dating and now his behavior had taken a turn that made us both worry that his attacks might turn physical.

"Are you sure you want to marry this dude?" I asked, adding that I thought she should get rid of him, the sooner the better. She thought for a moment, and I pictured the look that I knew so well, the one she always wore when she was worried, the one where a furrow would form between her brows and then her eyes would squint and her lips would tighten.

Finally she said, "Something's better than nothing." I couldn't ignore the fear and resignation I heard in her voice. My big sister had lost her only son to lupus the year before. Her loneliness was outweighing reason.

Less than a week after the call, Los Angeles was rocked by a powerful earthquake that was felt all the way to Oakland, where Joanne was living. She was home alone. A few days later, she set her wedding date.

I regret that I didn't go to the wedding. My house was broken into the week before and I wasn't comfortable leaving my two teenaged daughters there alone, or leaving the house unattended if they stayed with friends. Or maybe that was the excuse I told myself instead of admitting that I was afraid of flying or that I might say something to her new husband that would ruin her wedding or make her life more difficult after I left.

The day after the wedding, Tania and Ebony met me on the front porch on my way into the house after work. "You'd better sit down, Mom,"

Tania commanded, always the messenger. But before I could, she said "You need to call Jayne," my cousin in San Francisco. *Why was Jayne calling?* I wondered. Mama had flown to California for Joanne's wedding. *Why wasn't she the one who called? Had something happened to my mother?*

The girls led me into the house, stroking my hair and my shoulders as they escorted me to the three steps that led to the kitchen, the spot where I liked to sit when I just wanted to collect myself for a moment. When she thought I was ready, Tania brought me the phone.

"Joanne's in the hospital," said Jayne. "She had a brain aneurism. She's in a coma."

I wanted to talk to my mother. I wanted to hear her voice, to know how she was coping with this. My thoughts flew back to that August day eight years earlier, in 1984, the year of George Orwell's classic dystopian novel, back to the night

Mom called from Paris. Our beloved stepfather was in the American Hospital on the edge of life and my oldest brother, Woody, a multi-lingual man who had made a career as a communications specialist in the U.S. Army – my big brother who would succumb to a heart attack eleven years later – was on his way to help her. Mom and Barney had traveled to Paris to celebrate the blessing that his cancer had gone into remission. I still have a photo of them smiling under the marquee of Poisson et Boeuf, the restaurant where he contracted the food poisoning that would take him from us – food poisoning, not the cancer that we expected.

"Mom, how are you, Mama?" I begged when Jayne handed her the phone. "I'm fine," her standard reply for everything. But the flat, trance-like quality in her voice betrayed the numbness that

I knew she was feeling. She had been the mother of the bride the day before. Was she about to end the week at her daughter's funeral? Part of me wanted to jump on the next plane but I knew she was surrounded by our California family. They tended to ignore me when I was around them, or to somehow make me feel like I was in the way. I didn't relish being with them. Thankfully, Woody was there with Mama. I comforted myself by knowing that I was the one who would be here to give her the support she would need when she returned home.

It turned out to be a good thing that I didn't go to California. I caught a nasty flu the day after Jayne's call, the chills and fever, achy type that sends you to bed wondering if you will survive. The next afternoon while the girls were at school, I got up and slipped on my bathrobe and went downstairs to brew a cup of tea. I sat on the couch and watched whatever game show was on television, taking slow sips until the show went off, then put my cup in the sink and started back up the stairs. When I reached the halfway point, an odd feeling came over me. At first, I thought it was lightheadedness from the flu, but it felt different from that, it was something I hadn't experienced before. My body began to sway from side to side involuntarily and I gripped the railing and hung on for dear life. When the swaying stopped, I somehow knew that my sister had reached the moment when she had to decide whether to stay or to go. The two of us had always shared a symbiotic relationship, often knowing what each other needed or wanted without sharing any words, like twins are known to do. But we were not twins. Joanne was almost two years older than me. I sensed that she was reaching out, asking me to help her with this, perhaps her final decision. I stood on the stairs for a moment, wondering what to do. Then I asked her "What do you want to do?" Soon after I made my way up the stairs and back into my bed, Woody called.

Before Mama left San Francisco, Joanne's new husband found out that she had named our mother the beneficiary on her insurance policies. She died three days after their wedding, before she was able to revise her insurance policies and name John her beneficiary. And, really, who knows whether she intended to anyway? She had changed her beneficiary from her son to our mother after she recovered from that terrible loss. Maybe she simply wasn't ready to change it again. And maybe she didn't want to leave John with anything of hers that he could abuse.

John tried to bully Mom into turning the documents over to him, a campaign he continued after she returned to Minneapolis, calling her with intimidating words and threats. But little did he know my mother was not someone who cowered under pressure (when we were kids, we called her "The War Department"). Instead, she asked my uncle David, a lawyer, to look into John's background. We were sitting at her kitchen table having coffee when Uncle Dave called to tell her what he had learned: my sister's widower had three wives; two whom he had never divorced and one who had died under suspicious circumstances. Not wasting any time, Mama called John and warned him that unless he wanted this information exposed, he'd better leave her alone. She never heard from him again.

Instead of telling Cassandra what I was going through, I invited her to lunch. She had accepted, and now I stood at my door, fingers glued to the doorknob. The decision to take her to lunch had been easy because our phone conversation was so warm. "I've been thinking of you too," she had said.

I made reservations at Rainbow Chinese restaurant, a safe place where the staff knew me. Nevertheless, I took my time getting dressed, settling on colors that would calm me: a black turtleneck and a purple, brown and black scarf which I hoped would draw attention away from the uncertainty I was surely wearing on my face. I laced my boots and slung my bag over my shoulder, but when I got to the door, I couldn't move. What if my friends were right? What if the kindness I'd heard in the young woman's voice on the phone was a ruse to hide the truth – that she was really about to do me in? What would I do if her lawyer was with her? What if she was wearing a wire? Was I about to walk into something I wouldn't be able to get out of? Deciding that I had been watching too many "Law & Order" episodes, I turned the doorknob and walked down the hall, hoping there would be a note on the elevator announcing that it was out of service.

Once outside, I drove slowly through the cool, misty rain, stretching the twenty-minute drive to a half-hour. The soft rain fell rhythmically on my windshield like a heartbeat, seeming to echo my constant question – why am I still here? I have always believed that I was the least- favored child in our family. My relationship with my mother had always been troubled for reasons I may never understand. She seemed to be unusually hard on me, critical of my every move. I didn't make my bed right, didn't wash or dry the dishes well enough, didn't practice my piano lessons long enough and if I did, I didn't hit the notes properly. My grades would be so much better if I applied myself in school, she said, and on and on and on. I don't think she understood that I was a sensitive child, easily crushed by her unrelenting criticism. I fought back when I was a teenager and became a mother at the age of 17. Then she criticized me for getting pregnant and forced me to put my baby in foster care. I fought hard, and was allowed weekly, one-hour visits with my baby until the courts awarded me full custody on my eighteenth birthday. Then she criticized my lack of parenting skills. Later, after I married a man who beat me, she said it was my fault, then criticized me when I divorced him after giving birth to my fourth child. She had managed to take care of her four children after she and my biological father divorced, but she questioned my logic in escaping that marriage with four children to raise on my own.

One hot summer day when I was 33 and

pregnant with my fifth child, she came over with homemade cookies in hand, which she often did. I was sitting at my desk in my home office, where I operated a secretarial service, when I heard her voice. "Where's your mother?" I heard her ask whichever of my children answered the door. I remained seated when she stepped into my office, afraid that she would once again criticize me for having gotten pregnant, this time with an old boyfriend I took up with after my divorce. Instead, she stood silent for a moment. My mother was a stunning woman. Her beauty surprised me every time I saw her. She seemed especially beautiful that day, for reasons I didn't understand. Finally, she said something I never expected. She praised me for having broken the chain of child abuse that's been in our family for generations, something I didn't know until that moment. She didn't stop there. She then told me I had been born with a veil. "What's that?" I asked. If she responded, I don't remember, I was so shocked by her praise and this new information.

Later, the research I found said that one out of 80,000 babies is born with a veil, or "en caul," meaning they are born with their heads or their entire bodies still encased in the amniotic sac. In cultures that believe in superstitions or esoteric wisdom, a child born like this is said to have been born with a special destiny, or that they have psychic abilities, or are born with good luck. I've always felt like I was a bit strange, out of sync with most of the people around me. When I was a little girl, my mother frequently punished me because I looked at people as though I could see through them. Did she fear that she had given birth to a voodoo child? Her criticisms began to lessen after my sister passed away. Even moreso after we lost Woody.

All the way to the restaurant, I wondered if I would recognize Cassandra. Several weeks had passed since the accident and all I had was the memory of her rolling off the hood of my car and into the gutter, and the memory of sitting on the curb holding her head in my lap.

Once inside, I was comforted to see that my favorite bartender, Linnea, was working that day. Little did I know she would become my awesome Dean at Minneapolis Community & Technical College several years later. But back then she was taking a break from academe and was holding down an hourly-wage gig. Her welcoming smile left me feeling that whatever was going to happen that day, I would be all right.

The host greeted me and escorted me to the table where Cassandra was waiting. I recognized her right away. The short, dark curls I had stroked while waiting for the ambulance to arrive were unmistakable, but she seemed thinner than she had appeared on the night of the accident.

We made feeble attempts at small talk while perusing the menu. Apparently, small talk wasn't one of her talents either. Thankfully, the weather is always a passable topic in Minnesota, so we commented on the rain. When the server brought water and took our orders, we sat in uncomfortable silence, searching for words, both taking long glances at the restaurant's oversized goldfish tank and watching the lunch crowd slowly invade the popular restaurant. I ruminated briefly on another young woman named Cassandra, the character in Greek mythology who, like this girl sitting across the table from me, had curly dark hair and brown eyes. In the myth, Apollo was said to have given her the gift of prophecy, but later turned it into a curse that caused all who heard her prophecies to believe she was lying. I looked around the restaurant and didn't see anyone who looked suspiciously like a lawyer, nor did Cassandra appear to be wearing a wire, so I let my guard down, but only a little. We stared at each other for a brief moment, and I was relieved to see that, just as the police report had stated, she didn't seem to have endured any serious or permanent injuries from the accident.

I wanted to tell her how sorry I was for the harm I had caused her but was unable to find the words I had so carefully planned to say. Instead, she was the one who broke the silence. She cleared her throat, causing me to turn my attention from the goldfish tank and my heartbeat to rise in anticipation of what I feared she was about to say. Then she looked me in the eye and said, "You are an angel."

Her voice was as clear as her sharp brown

eyes. There was no mistaking what she had said, but I couldn't believe that I had heard her correctly. I had been worried sick about her and now here I was sitting across from her in this restaurant harboring a hint of a fear that she might reach into her purse and pull out a summons, or that two plainclothes detectives might walk over to us, one placing me in handcuffs while the other read me my Miranda rights. But instead, she had called me an angel!

The imaginary detectives slid out of the picture, but not before I could ask what she was thinking. "I could have killed you that night!"

She explained that she was a Mormon and had traveled here from her home state to be with a man she had fallen in love with, a guy who worked in theater.

"I have always loved theater," she said. A pained yet wistful look hovered over her face when she explained that her family was conservative and straight-laced and didn't approve of her aspirations toward the arts, fearing that it might disrupt her faith.

I don't know anything about the Mormon religion, but have certainly known Christians who have left family members feeling condemned and isolated for similar reasons. Also, I admit that as a parent, I have experienced moments when I feared what might happen to my children if they strayed away from the belief system I tried to instill in them. I do not follow a specific faith tradition but I do believe there is a Source higher than us who looks out for everyone, no matter their faith or their life orientations. So even though my beliefs are very different from those of her parents', I could understand their pain as well as hers.

A vague memory crossed my mind. Weren't the famous brother and sister duo, Donny and

Marie Osmond, Mormons? I was about to ask if her parents knew about them and their artistry, but before I could speak, I saw her eyes darken and a deep sadness seemed to envelop her like a cloak.

"Things didn't work out with the guy," she said. "I don't know if he changed or if he simply wasn't what I thought he was." I watched tears begin to creep down her pale cheeks and my thoughts returned to Cassandra of the Greek myth, whom Apollo cursed because she went back on her promise to be his lover. "He became mean, almost cruel in the things he said to me and after a while I lost confidence and began to feel confused."

She said that in spite of him, she enjoyed her time in Minneapolis. "I have met so many kind and wonderful people." She dried her tears with her napkin and said, "This was the first time I met people who were different from the people in my community back home. I had never seen people of different races, let alone lived next door to them or worked with them." Then after a brief pause she said, "But I miss my family and I have never stopped questioning my relationship with God."

She then looked me in the eye and said once again, "You are an angel."

She explained that until the accident, she didn't think she could go back home. She feared that she would be shamed and wouldn't be allowed back into her family or her church. "The accident helped me realize that I can go home." Then she thanked me for having been willing to be the messenger that gave her that clarity.

I hugged her and walked slowly out of the restaurant, still feeling a little dazed, but glad that I had followed my heart and had not allowed myself to be talked out of contacting her. I stood for a moment on the sidewalk in the misty rain then got back into my car.

All the way home, as the rain again echoed the beats of my heart, I thought about angels – some as messengers, others who come into our lives for brief periods of time, like my siblings and my beloved stepfather, the army of angels that I believe are always there guiding us, such as those who led me out of my troubled marriage and let me know that I could return home, and now the angels who brought Cassandra and me together to give her the same message. Maybe that is why I am still here. Maybe my siblings completed what they came here to do. Maybe I still have work to do.

coda

Two years before I celebrated my 50th birthday, I moved into the upper level of my parents' duplex. Not because they needed me – my stepfather had passed away some years before and Mom, a petite but tough and feisty lady in her 70s, was as strong as she had ever been. The move was the result of some unexpected financial problems that happened after I resigned from an untenable employment situation and was struck with a serious illness before I could find a new job. My severance, including my medical benefits, had dried up, leaving me with only a small, quickly-dwindling savings account.

My youngest daughter, 16-year-old Ebony, was the last of my five children still living at home. It was important to me that she continued to have a stable environment, but it was humiliating to be returning to my childhood home at an age when I should have been creating a comfortable space for my grandchildren. Nevertheless, I couldn't deny my good fortune. My parents' long-term tenants had purchased a home of their own and were moving out at the time that I had to vacate the place where I had been living.

The duplex, built in 1935 in a quiet, friendly neighborhood near Minnehaha Creek in south Minneapolis, is beautiful and spacious. A large picture window invites the sun into the living room during the day and entices the moon and stars to cast mysterious shadows at night. Hardwood floors that shine like honey stretch from the living and dining rooms all the way through to the three bedrooms, each as big as some of my friends' apartments, and a cozy breakfast nook nestles in the corner of the roomy kitchen.

One evening, a couple of months after we were settled in, I kissed my daughter goodbye and sent her off to whatever teenage thing she was doing that autumn night. It had been a long day of meetings and writing grant proposals for SASE: The Write Place, the new literary arts organization I was in the process of creating, and I was looking forward to a bit of solitude.

I slid a movie into the VHS player and slumped down on the sofa. I was about to dig into a bowl of freshly popped popcorn when I thought I saw something out of the corner of my eye. I didn't pay much attention, thinking it was my long-deceased maternal grandfather. He had been making periodic visits since my difficult pregnancy with Ebony, always showing up in the wheelchair he smiles from in the sepia photograph that has held a prominent place in my mother's home for as long as I can remember.

Feeling comforted that Grandfather Robert had stopped by to check on me again, I turned back to my popcorn and *Sleepless in Seattle*, which was about to begin. Suddenly, an odd, icy breeze passed through the room. I looked toward the door wondering if I had left it open a crack, and was taken aback to see a tall, stately woman standing there. She was dressed in a Victorian-era gown made of an expensive silken fabric woven in wide, vertical, black and antique gold stripes, and dainty buttons, covered in the same fabric, snaked up the bodice from her waist to her neck where a neckband, topped with fine lace, encircled her throat. A bustled skirt drifted from her tiny waist to the floor and long sleeves, puffed at the shoulders, hid her graceful arms. A large hat, enhanced with ostrich plumes, covered her thick, black pompadour. She was accompanied by a tall, dapper gentleman dressed in a tan suit and a top hat, and his arm was looped possessively through hers. I stared in disbelief, almost dropping my popcorn.

I was stunned by this ghostly intrusion, yet I somehow knew she was a relative, an ancestor. Fear and curiosity flooded over me as I wondered who she was and why she was there. She gazed at me with intense, dark eyes and then, as though responding to my thoughts, said, "I am Liza. You have to tell our story." And just like that, she and her gentleman were gone.

Visits from loved ones who have passed on were not new to me. Just the year before, my sister called on me to help her decide whether to stay or to cross over after she suffered a brain aneurism. Though she was in San Francisco and I was in

Minneapolis, I reached through the veil and held her hand, and knew the moment the aneurism took her life. Also, my beloved stepfather paid me a reassuring visit when I woke up from surgery shortly after he passed away in 1984. And, of course, there was Grandfather Robert. But this was the first time a spirit showed up with an explicit command.

Once I recovered and could breathe again, my mind was full of questions. Why was I the one she came to? What does she want me to say? What part(s) of my family's story want to be told, need to be told? Which stories will demand to be told? Who will be hurt by what I write? Who will be healed?

It was impossible to sleep that night, so when Ebony got home – a few minutes past her curfew – I told her what had happened. All three of my daughters are used to hearing my stories of ghostly visitations. But a visit from a spirit with a command was new. Ebony had questions that mirrored mine. So did daughters Iris and Tania when I told them the next day.

I knew I had no choice but to follow the command that had been given to me, but I didn't have a clue about where to begin. I thought that maybe my first step would be to try and find out who Liza was. The next day, I asked my mother if she knew of someone from our past named Liza. I was reluctant to share the reason for my question, fearing that she wouldn't believe me or would ridicule me for what she tended to characterize as my overactive imagination. Thankfully, she didn't ask, choosing only to tell me that she didn't know of anyone by that name.

I then called my cousin Stephanie and my stepmother Joyce, both of whom were genealogists. Joyce said she found a "Liza" in my father's ancestry. All she could give me was the name. She didn't know her story.

Cousin Stephanie, on the other hand, who also receives occasional visitations, said she had uncovered an "Eliza" in her research of my mother's side of the family: a slave who was living at the same time as the woman my stepmother had found. Eliza had lived on the plantation of John Lee, a contemporary of General Robert E. Lee. She somehow left the plantation and settled into a good life in Denver, Colorado, where she gave birth to my mixed-race Grandfather Robert, giving him the surname, Lee.

It is unclear whether she escaped after enduring sexual exploitation by this white man who held authority over his slaves, or if she was sold to someone in Colorado. Maybe she was

John Lee's mistress. From what we know of chattel slavery, either could have been true. It is no secret that many of our foremothers were raped at random, often repeatedly by the same man, and bore his children whom those men often denied. We also know that slaves were sold at the whim of the people whose "property" they were. But there are also stories of slave women and children who were taken care of by men who loved them.

Based on some of what I know about the history of my people, of my family's history, and also my own life, I started writing whatever came into my mind. After a while, stories began to form. Most writers are familiar with the muse who helps us with our writing and the critic who tries to put roadblocks in our path. For me, they are my two maternal aunts, both of whom had passed away many years ago. Sometimes, when I'm working on a difficult passage or trying to decide whether to tell the story I'm mulling over, I imagine my aunts sitting on my shoulders. The kindly and loving but judgmental one who held strong religious beliefs sits on my left shoulder, shaking her finger and saying, "Now don't you go stirring things up." My other aunt sits on my right shoulder, a cigarette in one hand and a glass of scotch in the other. She smiles encouragingly, "Don't hold back," she says. "Someone out there needs to hear what truth tellers have to say." It can be very difficult to find the balance between what to say and what to leave out, but I do the best I can.

Thankfully, I didn't have to live in Mom's home very long. Within a year, I was able to get back on my feet and move back into a home of my own, another sunny place with large windows and a beautiful view that inspired me to keep writing.

We lost my mother in 2013. She stated in her will that she wanted me sell her duplex and split the proceeds between myself, my stepbrother, and my niece. I moved back into her home once again, having decided to spend a year clearing things out and preparing the house to sell. Mom and my stepfather, Barney, had lived there for some 40 years, and cleaning it out would be a difficult task. But with my children and grandchildren's help, we managed to get it done.

One day when I was there alone going through family photos, I came across an old sepia photo that I had never seen before, a picture of a tall, stately woman dressed in a Victorian-era gown made of an expensive silken fabric woven in wide, vertical black and antique gold stripes.

Dainty buttons covered in the same fabric snaked up the bodice from her waist to her neck where a neckband, topped with fine lace, encircled her throat. A bustled skirt drifted from her tiny waist to the floor and long sleeves, puffed at the shoulders, hid her graceful arms. A large hat, enhanced with ostrich plumes, covered her thick, black pompadour. Her piercing eyes gazed out at me the same way they did that night twenty years before, and I could swear I saw her smile and nod at me with approval. I smiled back, feeling that maybe I was fulfilling her command.

Ever since the enslavement of my people began when the first known slave ship, the Man of War, docked in Jamestown, Virginia, in 1619, we have been sharing our stories through music, poetry, prose, drama, dance and other forms of art. The healing power of telling our stories cannot be stressed enough. This is what Liza demanded. And as we continue to share our stories, not only of pain, but also of the beauty and strength that has allowed us to survive, I am grateful to be able to include my voice.

Carolyn Holbrook is the founder and Artistic/ Executive Director of More Than a Single Story and SASE: The Write Place. Her essays have appeared most recently in *A Good Time For The Truth: Race in Minnesota* (MNHS Press) and *Blues Vision: African American Writing from Minnesota* (MNHS Press). Her book, *Ordinary People, Extraordinary Journeys: How the St. Paul Companies Leadership Initiatives in Neighborhoods Program Changed Lives and Communities* was published in 2015. She is also co-author of *Hope In the Struggle* (Univ. of MN Press), a memoir of Dr. Josie R. Johnson. She was the 2010 recipient of the MN Book Awards Kay Sexton Award and a 50 over 50 award from AARP and Pollen Midwest in 2016. In 2014 she won the Exemplary Teacher Award at Hamline University.

acknowledgments

Thank you to the women in my two writing groups – your support means the world to me.

Black Women Writing: Mary Moore Easter, Sherrie Fernandez-Williams, Carla-Elaine Johnson, Joan Maze, and Buffy Smith.

Women From the Center: Kyoko Katayama, Mai Neng Moua, Nora Murphy, Marcie Rendon, Jna Shelomith, Joan Trygg, and especially Diane Wilson, my longtime writing buddy.

Also to my awesome and incredibly fascinating children and grandchildren, and to my parents and siblings who have joined the ancestors.

And finally, to John Colburn for your amazing patience and feedback while working with me through the many drafts of these pieces. I am honored to have joined the cadre of weird writers you've been publishing since 1989.

MINNESOTA STATE ARTS BOARD

Carolyn Holbrook is a fiscal year 2015 recipient of an Artist Initiative grant from The Minnesota State Arts Board. This activity is made possible by the voters of Minnesota through a grant from the Minnesota State Arts Board, thanks to a legislative appropriation from the arts and cultural heritage fund.